NUMBERS AT PLAY!

The Math of **Games**

Written by Anne Rooney

WORLD BOOK

www.worldbook.com

Co-published by agreement between Shi Tu Hui and World Book, Inc.

Shi Tu Hui
Room 1807, Block 1,
#3 West Dawang Road
Chaoyang District, Beijing 100025
P.R. China

World Book, Inc.
180 North LaSalle Street
Suite 900
Chicago, Illinois 60601
USA

© 2026. All rights reserved. This volume may not be reproduced in whole or in part in any form without prior written permission from the publisher.

WORLD BOOK and the GLOBE DEVICE are registered trademarks or trademarks of World Book, Inc.

Library of Congress Control Number: 2025942099

Aha! Academy: Math
ISBN: 978-0-7166-7377-4 (set, hardcover)

Numbers at Play! The Math of Games
ISBN: 978-0-7166-7380-4 (hard cover)
ISBN: 978-0-7166-7443-6 (e-book)
ISBN: 978-0-7166-7433-7 (soft cover)

Staff

Editorial

Vice President
Tom Evans

Editorial Project Coordinator
Kaile Kilner

Senior Curriculum Designer
Caroline Davidson

Curriculum Designer
Mikayla Kightlinger

Proofreader
Nathalie Strassheim

Indexer
Nathaniel Lindstrom

Graphics and Design

Senior Visual Communications Designer
Melanie Bender

Designer
Shannon Hagman

Written by Anne Rooney

Designed by Starletta Polster

Acknowledgments

The publishers gratefully acknowledge the following sources for photography. All illustrations were prepared by WORLD BOOK unless otherwise noted.

Cover: FREEPIK2/Shutterstock; Gilmanshin/Shutterstock; kmls/Shutterstock; Roman Samborskyi/Shutterstock; Vlad Antonov/Shutterstock

© Carlo Bollo/Alamy 19; © GL Archive/Alamy 35; © Science History Images/Alamy 23; Public Domain 31; © Shutterstock 4, 5, 6, 7, 8, 9, 10, 11, 12, 13, 14, 15, 16, 17, 18, 19, 20, 21, 22, 23, 24, 25, 26, 27, 28, 29, 30, 31, 32, 33, 34, 35, 36, 37, 38, 39, 40, 41, 42, 43, 44, 45, 46, 47, 48; Wellcome Collection (CC BY 4.0) 9

There is a glossary of terms on page 48. Terms defined in the glossary are in type that looks like *this* on their first appearance on any spread (two facing pages).

Contents

Introduction 4

① **What are the chances?** 6

    Heads or tails? 8
    A roll of the dice 10
    Winning the lottery 12
    Really random? 14
    Cars and goats 16

② **No chance!** 18

    All in a row .20
    Your move! .22
    Making the most of chances 24
    Fair play 26

③ **All fair and square** 28

    It's magic! 30
    Squares without the magic 32
    Squares and ships 34
    Keeping score 36

④ **Bits and bytes of math** 38

    Extra dimensions 40
    Math makes the wind blow! 42

Dueling digits! .44
Index 46
Glossary 48

Introduction

Do you like to play games? You probably don't think of games as math, but there's tons of math in games. Often, you don't even notice it, but those sneaky numbers and patterns are everywhere!

Every time you roll a die, you're playing a game with math. Games as simple as tic-tac-toe, as complex as chess, and as exciting as online adventure games all use math. Obviously, you use math to keep score—but there's math in making patterns, predicting events, and weighing up chances. It's a great reason to spend your time playing games—you're secretly learning math!

 WHAT ARE THE CHANCES?

The chance, or *probability*, of an event is important in games and in real life. Many games involve some element of chance—flipping a coin, tossing a die, or spinning a wheel.

What are the chances you will win in the raffle at the school fair? Or that you will throw a double six with two dice? Or that you will be picked for the football team?

It's just luck whether you pick a duck with a winning number.

Some events are truly *random*: every ticket in the raffle has the same probability of winning. But whether you will be picked for the football team depends on how good you are at football and the standard of the other players.

In games of pure chance you can't change the likelihood of winning. You can't be good at these games! But they can still be fun and it's cool to see the math lurking beneath the surface—so let's take a look.

A game like Snakes and Ladders, called Hounds and Jackals, was played in ancient Egypt!

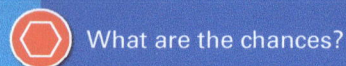

What are the chances?

Heads or tails?

To work out the *probability* of something happening, we divide the number of ways something can happen by the total number of possible outcomes. A coin can fall two ways, and heads is one of them, so the chance of heads is 1 in 2. Probabilities can also be written as fractions: 1 in 2 is the same as ½ because the event will happen half the time. We can also write it as 0.5 or 50%. They all mean the same thing.

A coin will land heads about half the time. But if you toss a coin 10 times it probably won't come down heads five times and tails five times. Each toss of the coin is independent—the result of one toss doesn't affect the next. You *could* get 10 heads in a row!

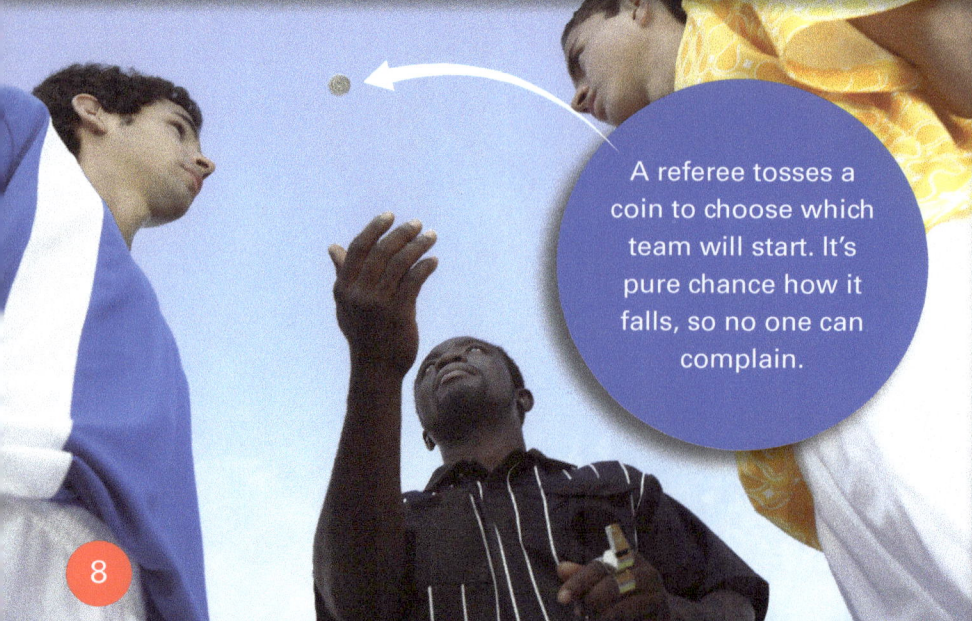

A referee tosses a coin to choose which team will start. It's pure chance how it falls, so no one can complain.

A tossed coin can come down heads or tails. The chances of each are 1 in 2 because there are only two options. Mathematicians call this probability.

If we play more than once, we multiply the probabilities together. The probability of getting heads twice is ¼ (½ × ½). The chance of heads three times in a row is ⅛ (½ × ½ × ½). The chance of getting heads 10 times is 1 in 2,048. You can't depend on your luck staying the same or changing!

The chances of five coins all coming down heads is 1 in 2^5 (2 × 2 × 2 × 2 × 2 = 32)

The chance of 35 coins all coming down heads is less than 1 in 34 *billion*!

Italian mathematician **Gerolamo Cardano** wrote the first book about probability around 1564. Cardano was short of money, which led him to investigate the odds of winning at games of dice. His math meant he won often enough to survive!

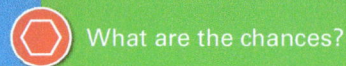

What are the chances?

A roll of the dice

A die has six sides, so there is an equal chance of getting any number, 1–6. There's just the same chance of throwing a 6 as throwing a 1 or a 3, even if it doesn't seem like it when you play!

Throwing two dice, there are 36 (6 × 6) possible combinations, giving scores between 2 and 12—but the chances aren't equal for all scores. There's only one way to score 2 or 12, but there are six ways of scoring 7. That means 7 happens most.

CAREER CORNER

Risk management professionals calculate the chances of bad events, such as floods or earthquakes. Then they figure out whether improving a building to make it earthquake-proof, say, is worth the money, or whether the risk is too low to worry about.

Throw a six to start... Throw a double to take an extra turn... Lots of games rely on throwing dice.

The game Sevens makes use of how often you can throw 7 with two dice. Each player throws six dice, then removes any pairs that make 7. For example, if you threw 4, 5, 2, 1, 2, 3, you would remove 4 + 3 and 5 + 2. This leaves 1 + 2, giving you a score of 3. You could then choose whether to keep this score or throw again to try for a higher score. Although what you get is pure chance, knowing that you are likely to get a score higher than 3 if you throw again is useful information!

People have played dice for thousands of years!

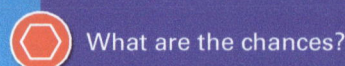

What are the chances?

Winning the lottery

The more raffle tickets you have, the better your chance of winning, but it doesn't matter *which* tickets you have. Every ticket has the same chance of winning. If there are 100 tickets and you buy one, you have a 1 in 100 chance (0.01, or 1%). If you buy 10 tickets, you have a 10/100 chance, which is 1/10 (0.1, or 10%).

In a lottery, people choose several numbers. They win the big prize if all their numbers come up. What are the chances?

Yay! I won!

In carnival games of chance, you are always more likely to lose than to win!

TECH TIME

Computers use *random* numbers in *encrypting data*—to generate the *security key*s used in making secure bank payments and contracts. They often start from numbers generated from random atmospheric "noise" or *radioactive decay*.

Do you want to win a giant teddy bear or a tablet computer? You might buy a raffle ticket. A lottery or a raffle is entirely a game of chance.

Suppose a lottery draws six numbers, each of which is 1–60. The chance of one of your numbers coming up first is 6 in 60, or 1 in 10, which is 0.1. That doesn't sound too bad.

The chance of another number coming up is 5 in 59, or 0.085, as you have 5 numbers left and there are now 59 to choose from (there were 60, but one has been removed). The chance of getting both numbers is 0.1 × 0.085 = 0.0085.

	Chance	Probability	% probability
First number	6 in 60	0.1	10 %
Second number	5 in 59	0.085	8.5 %
Third number	4 in 58	0.069	6.9 %
Fourth number	3 in 57	0.053	5.3 %
Fifth number	2 in 56	0.036	3.6 %
Sixth number	1 in 55	0.018	1.8 %

The *probability* of getting all six numbers is 0.1 × 0.085 × 0.069 × 0.053 × 0.036 × 0.018, or around 1 in 50 million. You are ten times more likely to be killed by a shark!

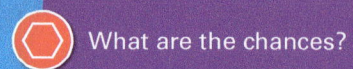 What are the chances?

Really random?

It's actually very difficult to pick completely random numbers. If someone asks you to pick three numbers, you might think you are choosing randomly, but **subconscious** ideas will influence your choice. You probably won't pick 1, 2, 3 as they don't look random!

1   2   3

1, 2, 3, 4, 5, 6

Yet when numbers are chosen truly randomly, the sequence 1, 2, 3, 4, 5, 6 is as likely or unlikely as any other set of six numbers. If you choose those numbers in a lottery, and they come up, you probably won't have to share the prize with anyone else!

Generating random numbers by computer is very difficult because a computer must follow the rules of its programming, and rules tend to lead to predictable results.

Lotteries often use machines that tumble numbered balls in a drum and drop six randomly.

A lottery must pick entirely *random numbers* with no preference for particular numbers, or it wouldn't be fair. But how easy is that?

Many things that look random—such as a random playlist or random selection from a photo album—are only *pseudo-random*: they look random but aren't really. If they were really random, you could get the same track three times in a row, which people would complain wasn't random!

There are lots of online random tools—even random bird generators!

True randomness comes from physical states and events, like the roll of a die.

 ## CURIOUS CONNECTIONS

CHEMISTRY In a radioactive substance, any atom can decay (change its composition) at any moment. There's no way of predicting it, and it's entirely random. **Radioactive decay** can be used to produce random numbers.

What are the chances?

Cars and goats

Imagine a game show in which you can choose to open one of three doors to win a prize. Two doors hide goats, but one hides a car. You choose door #1. The host opens door #3 to reveal a goat. Now there are two closed doors, one of which hides a goat and one of which hides a car.

You can now switch your choice to the other closed door. Do you have a better chance of winning the car if you switch?

DID YOU KNOW?

There's a lot of *psychology* involved in how we think about probability. If you have a 1 in 5 chance of winning a prize, you will probably buy a raffle ticket. But if you have a 1 in 5 chance of being hurt if you try a trick, you probably won't try it! We weigh up the good and the bad as well as the numbers.

Probability doesn't always stay the same—it can change as a game unfolds. A famous example called the Monty Hall Problem shows this.

Most people will say no, the chance of winning is now 1 in 2 as there are only two doors left. But mathematicians show switching improves your chances to 2 in 3! Here's how it works if you originally choose door #1:

Behind door 1	Behind door 2	Behind door 3	Result if staying at door #1	Result if switching to the other closed door
goat	goat	car	goat	car
goat	car	goat	goat	car
car	goat	goat	car	goat

There was a 2 in 3 chance at the start that the car was behind another door. The probability is still the same—you can now just rule out one door, so the other has the 2 in 3 chance.

When the show host opens another door, he is filtering the remaining doors—he's removed one of the 1-in-3 chances. Imagine there were 100 doors. Your first pick has a 1-in-100 chance of being right. The chances you had picked the right door are slight, but the host has information you don't. He's now removed lots of bad choices you could make. Just like in life, getting more information is a good thing. It helps you to make a better decision.

2 NO CHANCE!

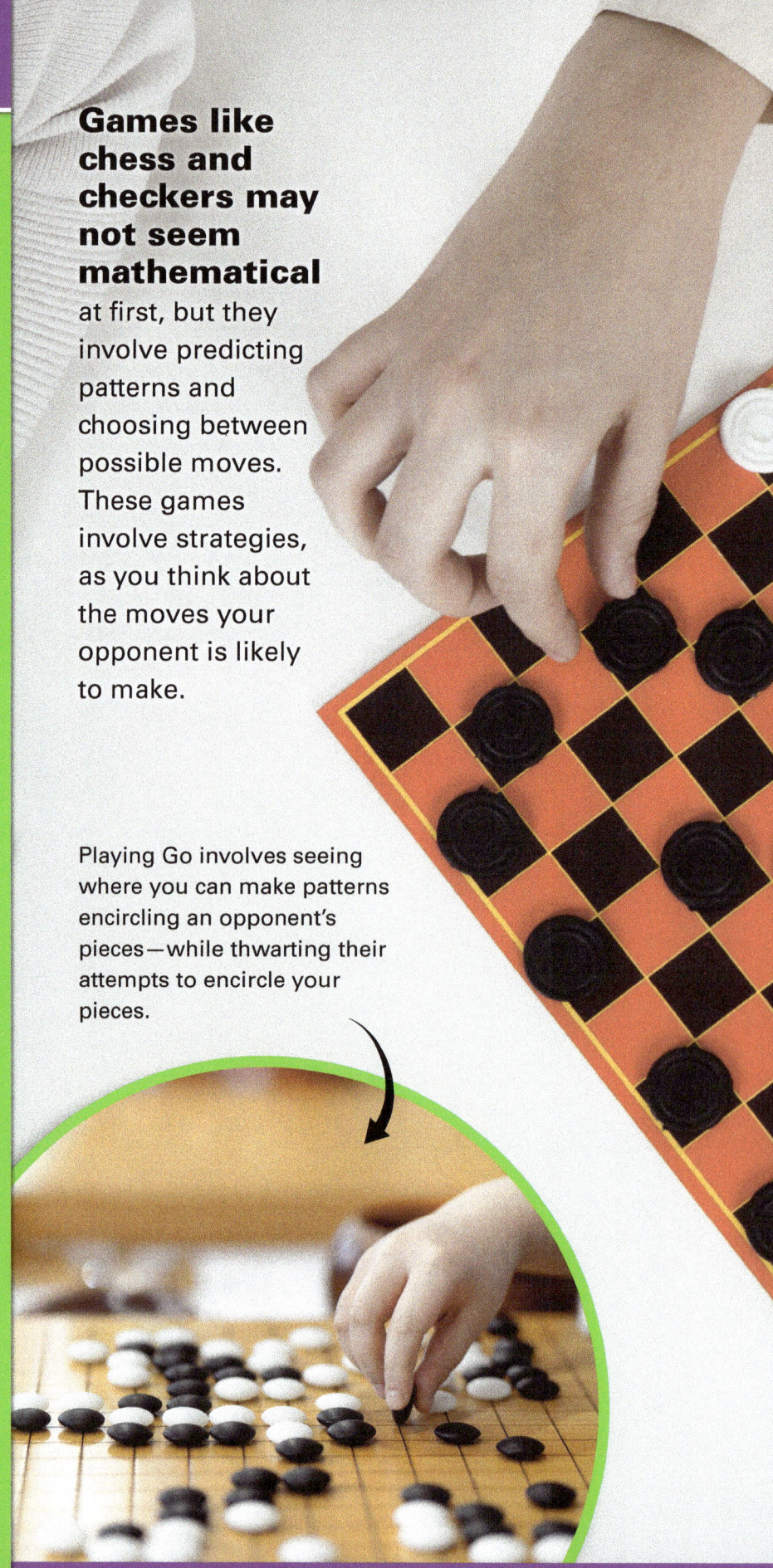

Games like chess and checkers may not seem mathematical at first, but they involve predicting patterns and choosing between possible moves. These games involve strategies, as you think about the moves your opponent is likely to make.

Playing Go involves seeing where you can make patterns encircling an opponent's pieces—while thwarting their attempts to encircle your pieces.

The opposite of a game of chance is a game of skill. Many games involve elements of both.

You have to think ahead, anticipate good and bad moves, and work out what they will mean for your next move or the one after. Then you will have to think about how likely each move is, so there's some *probability*.

There can be a lot of mathematical thinking in games of strategy and skill—even in a game that looks as simple as tic-tac-toe! Read on to see how math can help you win!

What will he do next?

In *Jenga*, you have to work out if the blocks will fall!.

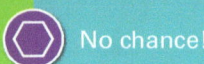 No chance!

All in a row

Two players take turns to write an X or O in a three-by-three grid. The first to get a full line of symbols wins.

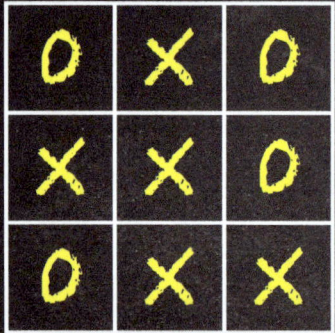

You need to look ahead to see what each move makes possible: you need to block your opponent and move towards your own line of three. It's all about seeing patterns.

The best first choice is the middle square.

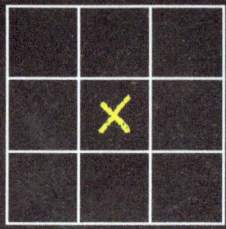

This gives you a start on any of four possible lines:

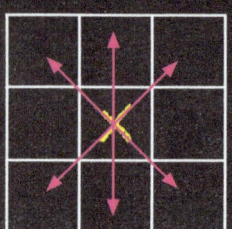

A mark in a corner or side gives you a start on only two possible lines:

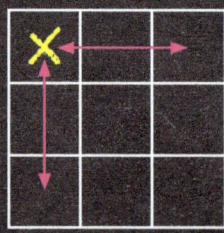 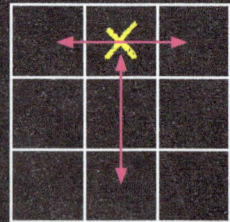

If you're going second, any square will help to block your opponent in one direction, but a corner gives you a start in two directions. The middle of a side gives you a chance at only one line:

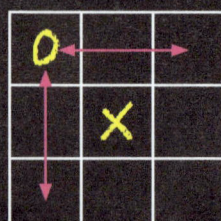 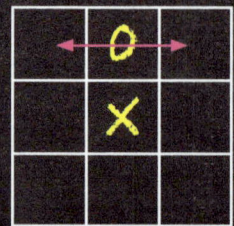

You've probably played tic-tac-toe without ever thinking about the math involved—but it's there!

Here, Player 2 has no choice but to place their O in the bottom right corner, or Player 1 will win.

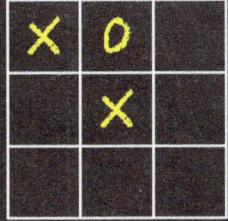

But this move doesn't get Player 2 any closer to winning, just a step away from losing.

The game is much harder with a larger grid!

Four-in-a-row takes even more pattern-spotting and thinking ahead.

The oldest known game of **tic-tac-toe** is from ancient Egypt! It was found scratched into roof tiles dating from 1300 B.C.—so 3,500 years ago! Romans also played it, calling it "terni lapilli," which means "pinches of pebbles."

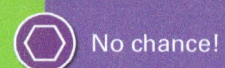 No chance!

Your move!

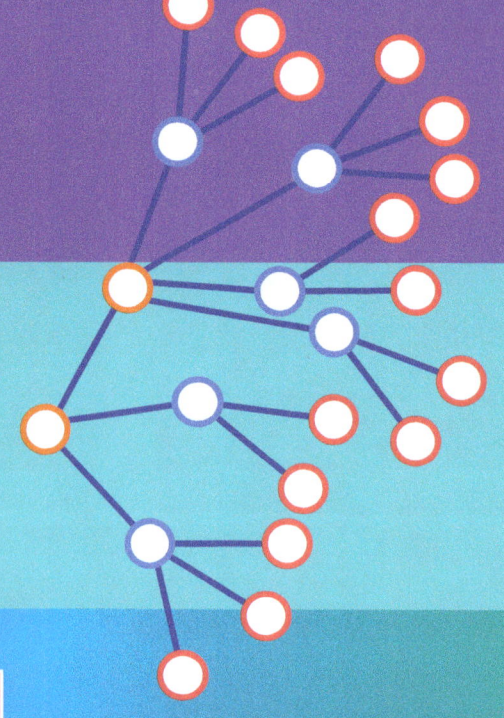

Each move opens up a host of possible later moves for you and your opponent. These stretch into a *game tree* of different ways the game could go. At each step, the tree gets more branches.

Imagine a tic-tac-toe grid on which you could place nine different symbols—perhaps the numbers 1-9. There are 9 places you can put the first symbol, then for each option there are 8 possibilities for the next symbol, making 9 × 8 = 72 possibilities for the first two moves. Then there are 7 places left for the next symbol, 6 for the one after, and so on. This means the total number of possible arrangements is

9 × 8 × 7 × 6 × 5 × 4 × 3 × 2 × 1 = 362,880.

Mathematicians call this nine *factorial* and write it "9!"

In tic-tac-toe, there are only two symbols: X will appear five times and O four times, so the number of arrangements drops to:

$$\frac{9!}{5! \times 4!} = 126$$

(Many games are actually the same, just viewed from a different direction. Removing these, leaves only 23 different games.)

The number of possible moves in a game like chess is mind-boggling!

A game like chess has many, many more options. There are at least 10^{120} possible games—that's 1 followed by 120 zeroes! And there are around 10^{360} possible games of Go.

A game tree for tossing a coin doubles the possibilities for the game with each toss.

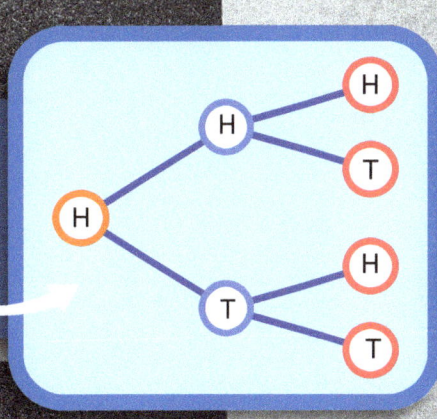

American mathematician **Claude Elwood Shannon** (1916–2001) worked in code-breaking during World War II and helped develop the math computers use. He was the first person to consider programming a computer to play chess. He calculated the possible number of chess games, called the Shannon Number.

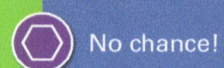
No chance!

Making the most of chances

Players "buy" squares on the board, develop property on them, then charge "rent" from players who land on the squares.

There is a lot of strategy in Monopoly, and it's all based in math. Some squares are cheap to buy but yield a low rent, while others cost more but bring in more rent. Players must choose between costly investments, possibly with high rewards, or low investments with lower rewards.

Would you like a house on Park Place?

You could buy it in Monopoly, a board game about buying and selling real estate.

"You owe me!"

Players need to think before over-stretching themselves, buying too much and leaving themselves little money to spare. If they are hit with a bill in the game that they can't pay, they might lose or they might have to take out a loan. They have to pay back the loan with *interest*, just as in real life. What would you do? Try to buy as much as possible, or be more cautious? Why?

CAREER CORNER

Real-world investors have to make the same kind of choices and predictions as players of Monopoly. Will they buy something that will yield a little money quickly, or more over a longer term? How much should they invest? What are the risks? They work with *probability* and with looking at patterns in how an investment has performed in the past.

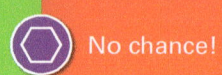 No chance!

Fair play

Game theory deals with the effects of other people on probabilities and outcomes. Suppose someone gives you $100 and asks you to give some to another player. You can choose how much to give, if any. They will receive triple the amount—so if you give $20, they receive $60. They can then give some back to you in the same way. If you give nothing, you will have $100. If you give generously, you may end up with more than $100—or less.

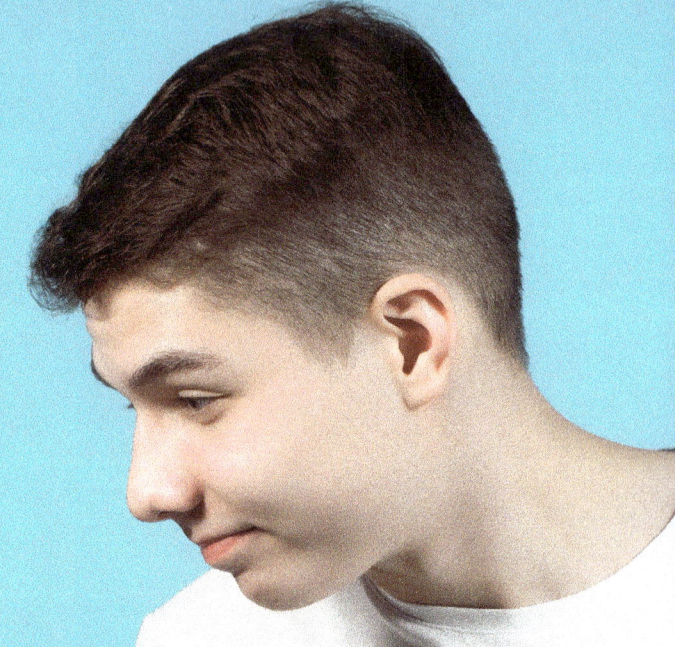

In experiments, people generally do give. They trust others to act well if they act nicely first, and it seems to happen.

Owww!

Game theory informs all kinds of conflict, from war and business to simple fights.

Most games are played with other players. This means you often need to think about what other players are thinking—but you can't see inside their heads!

Mathematicians discuss another game, called the Prisoner's Dilemma. Two criminals who worked together are separately offered a deal: if one betrays the other, they will go free but their partner will go to jail. If both stay silent, they will both go to jail for a shorter time. The best bet for each is to betray their partner because that's the only way of avoiding a long sentence, and they might go free.

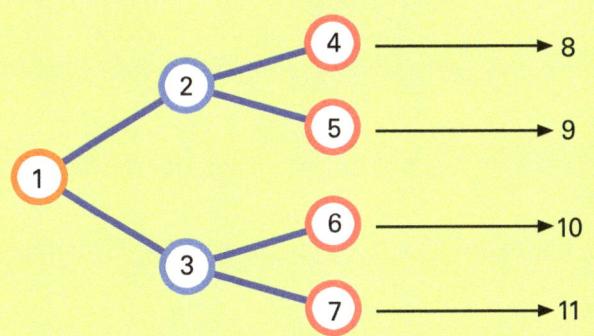

1. Criminal A questioned
2. Criminal A silent
3. Criminal A talks
4. Criminal B silent
5. Criminal B talks
6. Criminal B silent
7. Criminal B talks
8. Criminal A&B: short sentence
9. Criminal B: free; A: long sentence
10. Criminal A: free, B: long sentence
11. Criminal A&B: medium sentence

How do you think you would respond in these situations? Your own thoughts, feelings, and values affect your decisions in life and in games. You might not do what most people do.

CURIOUS CONNECTIONS

ENVIRONMENTAL SCIENCE

Experimental games like this have an impact on real-world situations. To avoid catastrophic climate change, all countries must reduce their carbon emissions. But each country suspects others won't do so, and those one that do will be disadvantaged financially—no one wants to go first.

3 ALL FAIR AND SQUARE

A grid can start empty and be filled in by players during the game, as it is in tic-tac-toe. Or it can be a field on which a game is played, like in chess or Go. A larger grid (with more squares) offers more possible moves or solutions.

In a game of strategy like chess and checkers, you use the squares to move pieces and try to trap your opponent's pieces. You need to think about the paths you can make across the board using allowed moves.

The squares of a grid are the background for many games, from tic-tac-toe to chess and checkers.

Hmmm, what now?

A checkers board has 64 black and white squares.

Go uses the lines around the squares, placing stones on the intersections (crossing points). Like chess and checkers, it's a game of strategy, but the pieces don't move. You have to think about patterns rather than paths.

Go has 19 squares in each direction—a total of 19 × 19 = 361 squares. There are 2 × 10^{170} possible arrangements (2 followed by 170 zeroes).

Even tic-tac-toe gets really complicated with a very large grid!

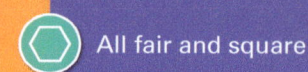

All fair and square

It's magic!

If you want a challenge, you can try making a magic square. It's a grid with a different number in each cell, but all the rows, columns and diagonals add up to the same total. This is a very old type of math game—at least 5,000 years old.

2	7	6	→ 15
9	5	1	→ 15
4	3	8	→ 15

15 15 15 15 15

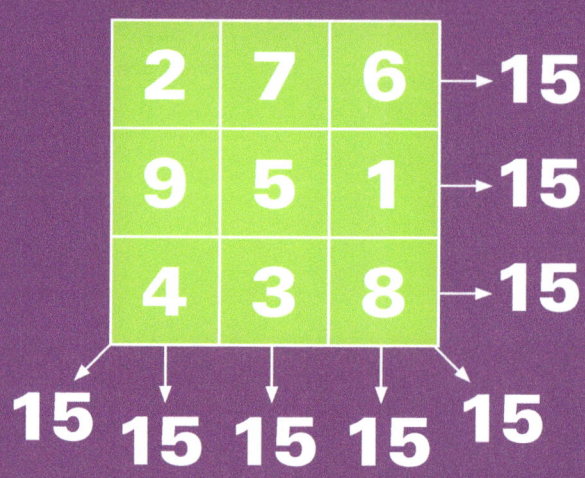

This is only one solution for the smallest magic square, a grid three by three (so nine squares in total). Other "solutions" are simply the same pattern rotated or reflected.

The squares of a grid lend themselves to games in arithmetic and math patterns.

Squares with four rows and columns (16 cells) are also common. The rows all total 34—and there are 880 different solutions! Larger squares are much more difficult to make, but also have many more solutions. There are 275,305,224 solutions to a 5 × 5 square—and possibly more than 17 million trillion solutions to a 6 × 6 square. There's a challenge to keep you awake at night!

5 × 5 square

6 × 6 square

Legend tells that when the river Lo in China flooded, people prayed and their gods sent a turtle with a magic square on its back as a sign. It was the simplest there is: **nine cells**, with spots adding up to each of the digits 1-9.

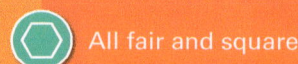

All fair and square

Squares without the magic

There are no sums in *sudoku*. The math here is working out how to complete the pattern. The numbers aren't used as numbers at all—it works just as well with letters or little pictures as with numbers 1-9.

A sudoku puzzle is a grid of grids, like this:

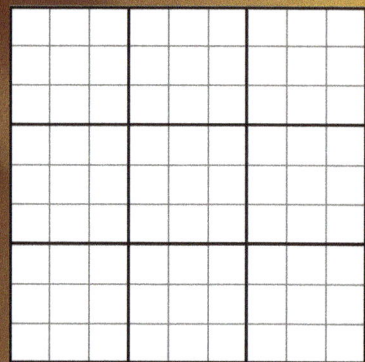

The challenge is to fill in the grid using each digit, 1-9, only once in each small grid, and in each long horizontal row, and in each long vertical column. The numbers don't need to add up. A sudoku puzzle has some numbers filled in, and you need to work out the rest.

An easy puzzle has lots of numbers in place.

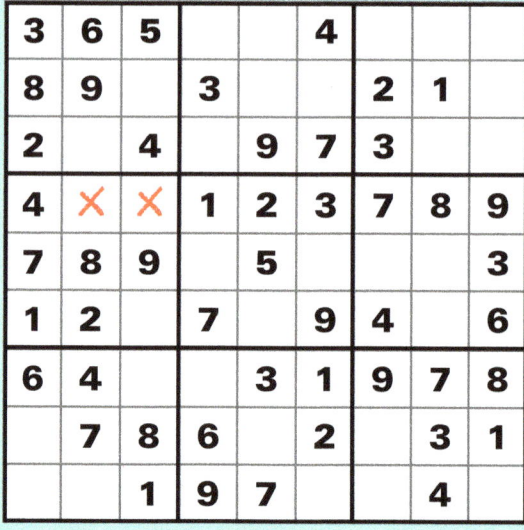

In row 4 here, only 5 and 6 are missing.

Column 2 already has a 6 and column 3 already has a 5, so this row must be:

| 4 | 5 | 6 | 1 | 2 | 3 | 7 | 8 | 9 |

32

Patterns and arrangements are also math! Lots of grid puzzles need you to think through patterns.

In a magic 15 puzzle you have to slide one number at a time to move all the numbers into order, 1-15. Half the possible starting positions are unsolvable!

3D puzzles come in lots of shapes!

Any Rubik's cube puzzle can be solved in 22 moves or fewer!

A Rubik's cube is a grid puzzle in three dimensions. To make each face a single color takes lots of planning and fiddling!

DID YOU KNOW?

There's only one solution to a sudoku puzzle set in a book or magazine—but there are 6,670,903,752,021,072,936,960 (more than 6 sextillion) possible solutions to sudoku!

All fair and square

Squares and ships

Players secretly position ships of different sizes and shapes on a grid, then each player tries to work out where their opponent's ships are.

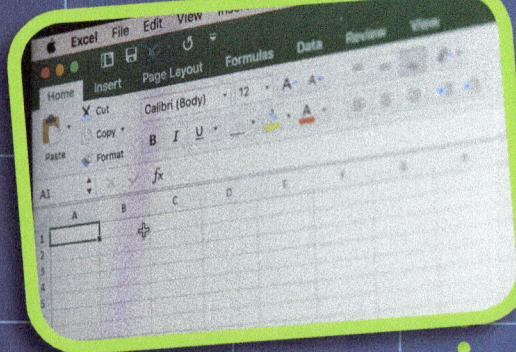

Each cell is identified by a letter and number. These are its *coordinates*—they work like an address. The first cell is A1. The cell below it is B1, and so on. We use the same system in a spreadsheet.

Each player has the same number and type of ships, and each type has a fixed size and shape. For example, a battleship might be five squares long, and a cruiser four squares long.

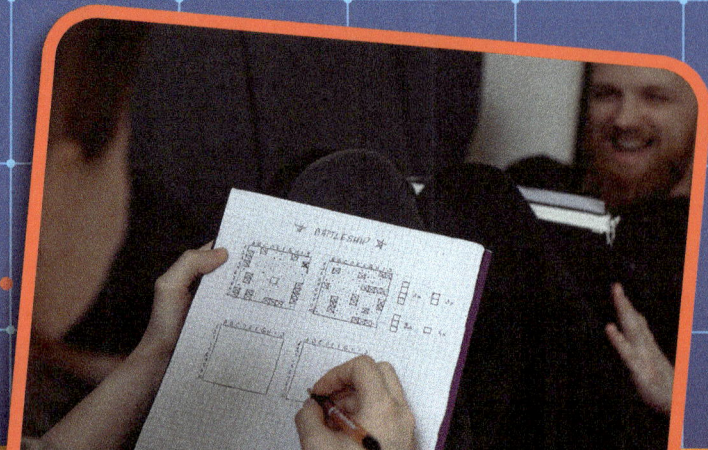

The game Battleship uses a grid to hide patterns. You have to puzzle out what can be where!

Players take turns to call out a grid reference and discover whether it's a "hit" (occupied) or a "miss" (empty). You must hit all squares occupied by a ship to sink it, and sink all your opponent's ships to win.

To win, you need to work out a strategy for finding ships. You might target the middle, or every other square. You have to think about how your opponent's ships could be arranged—and how best to position yours!

One down here…

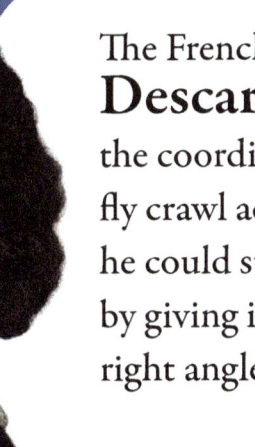

The French mathematician **René Descartes** is said to have invented the coordinate system after watching a fly crawl across his ceiling. He realized he could state the fly's exact position by giving its distance from two walls at right angles to each other.

 All fair and square

Keeping score

In Scrabble, players make words by placing letter tiles on a grid, like a crossword. Each letter has a score, and the score for a word is the total of the letter scores. But look out for squares that increase the value of a letter or word!

A lot of math has gone into designing the game. The letter scores and numbers of each tile are based on how common the letters are, which varies between languages. The letter scores in Spanish won't be the same as in English!

The most common letters have a score of 1. There are most of these tiles and they are easiest to place. Uncommon letters score up to 10. There are fewest of these tiles.

Beside *arithmetic*, you practise pattern recognition and strategy as you try not to leave good opportunities for your opponents.

Many games need you to keep score by **adding up,** and some have more complicated bits of scoring!

Darts also has complex score keeping. You work back from a total of 301 or 501 to exactly zero. High and low areas are mixed up, and there are thin rings of double and triple scores. You need to be quick at arithmetic!

Playing *hangman*, you use what you know about the frequency and patterns of letters to make guesses based in *probability*.

TECH TIME

AI programs that generate text work on word frequency. They sample lots of text and work out which words usually follow others. That's how a phone offers to complete words and phrases for you in a text message.

4
BITS AND BYTES OF MATH

Most of us enjoy computer games, and they feel like pure fun. But they are also pure math!

None of those monsters, heroes, building blocks or swords actually exists—they are all built from numbers and computer code. They are then animated—made to move—through the three-dimensional imagined world of the game. There's lots of math under the hood that you never see!

Adventure and *simulation* games have a branching structure—if you take path A, event X happens, but if you take path B, event Y happens. (You'll remember this from *game trees*.) These are all structured with math. The game has nearly endless possibilities, opening up new worlds and storylines with each choice. You might not be thinking about numbers when you play, but someone did a lot of math to get it working!

Some scientists think reality might be a multiverse, with new alternative universes branching off each time we make a choice.

Bits and bytes of math

Extra dimensions

When your character flies through space, when you build a towering castle, or race a car around a virtual circuit, you are playing in three dimensions of space—and one of time.

Older computer games are two-dimensional. You move over a flat surface, going up and down, left, and right. Two *coordinates* specify any point in the scene, measuring the distance from the edges of the game's world. Your moves are changes of coordinates.

More complicated games are three-dimensional. Your character can move through 3D space, going up, down, left, right, and "into" and "out of" the screen. Games like Minecraft, Zelda, Planet Zoo, and hosts of others work in 3D. Points in three dimensions have three coordinates: X, Y, and Z.

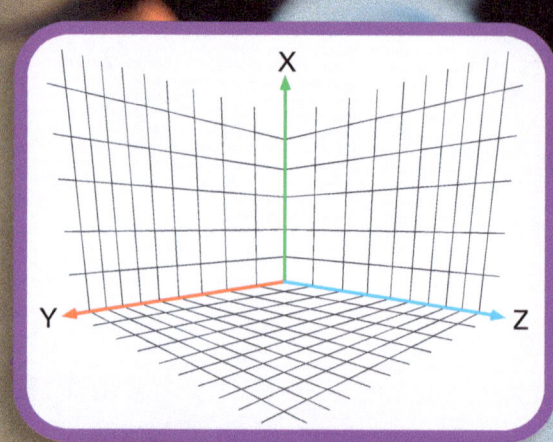

Virtual worlds are multidimensional,
just like reality—and math!

A computer game is also lit by numbers.

Math works out how light will shine from a source at a specific location, which might even be outside the scene, and illuminate objects. This technique is called "ray tracing." It involves working out the path taken by each ray of light as it moves across the scene, reflecting off surfaces, being blurred by smoke or clouds, casting shadows, and making light and dark areas. If a candle or lantern flickers, the lighting changes constantly.

CAREER CORNER

Architects visualize new buildings and even towns in the same way as computer games make fantasy scenes. They build a 3D world using math which people can move around in to explore what the space will be like.

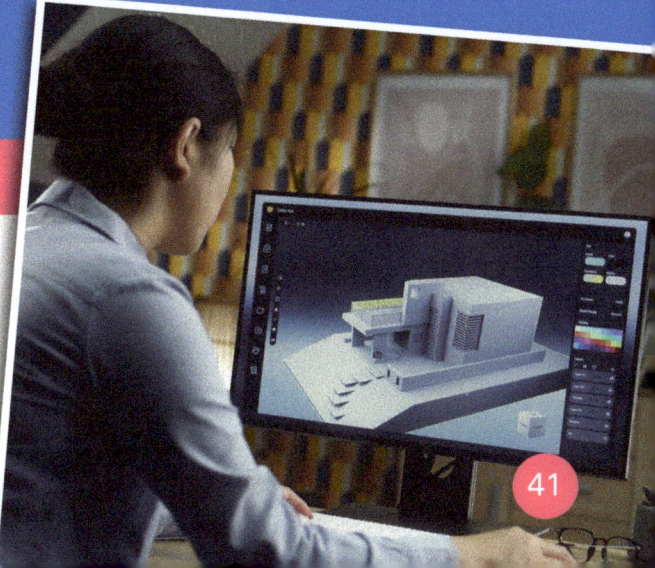

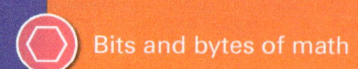
Bits and bytes of math

Math makes the wind blow!

Scenery and characters in a game move and change all the time. Time is a fourth dimension that games developers have to calculate with.

Some games have more realistic visuals than others, but all involve moving through time and space.

In games with simple graphics, like Minecraft, blocky characters and scenes have a restricted set of movements. Each time you make a character run, it runs in the same way. The same math is used each time.

I make only simple moves!

The wind blows in the trees, rocks fall down a mountain, water flows in the river, and fire destroys a city—all created by math!

Realistic movements can be created using an actor wearing a motion capture (mocap) suit. It captures the **coordinates** of individual points on a body part as it moves through space. The computer uses the traced movements to move equivalent points on the animated game character. The character is moved against a background scene.

Realistic characters and scenery are created by first making a wireframe or mesh and then draping surface textures and colors over it. The whole object can then be moved, looked at from different angles, or viewed in different lighting—all using math.

DID YOU KNOW?

The same techniques and math used to make realistic movement for games characters can help us work out how extinct animals moved! *Motion capture data* from living animals can be used to work out from fossilized bones how such animals as dinosaurs moved in the past.

43

Dueling digits!

You will need:
- Deck of cards
- Partner

Give it a try

1. Go through the deck of cards and take out any face cards (jacks, queens, kings, aces).
2. Shuffle the cards and divide them into two equal piles.
3. Each player should have their card pile face down in front of them.
4. For each round, players will flip over one card from their pile at the same time and try to be the first one to add together the digits on the cards and yell out the sum.
5. Whichever player yells out the correct answer first wins the cards and takes both cards to add to their pile.

For example: If one player lays down a 7 and the other lays down a 4 and the operation is addition, the first player to yell out 11 wins the cards.

Ready for an epic battle of numbers? Grab a deck of cards, a friend or family member, and prepare to put your mental math skills to the test. Only one mathematician can win. Will it be you?

6. If players yell out the same sum at the same time, it's time for a duel! Lay out 3 cards face down and flip the last one at the same time as their partner. Whoever yells out the sum of those cards first wins all the cards used in the duel.

7. The game is over when one player has acquired all the cards in the game.

Try this next!

Have you mastered addition? Challenge yourself by playing the game with subtraction or multiplication next. For subtraction, make sure to establish whose card will be the first digit in the equation, be ready for some negative numbers!

QUESTION TIME!

What is the greatest sum possible in this game? How about the smallest? If you played with multiplication, what is the greatest possible product? What would be the smallest?

Index

A
adventure games, 5, 39
architecture (career), 41
arithmetic, 31, 36-37
artificial intelligence (AI), 37
atmospheric noise, 13

B
Battleship (game), 35

C
Cardano, Gerolamo, 9
cards, 44-45
checkers, 18, 28-29
chemistry, 15
chess, 5, 18, 23, 28
China, 31
climate change, 27
coin tossing, 6, 8-9, 23
computer code, 23, 38
computer games, 38-43
coordinates, 34-35, 40, 43

D
darts (game), 37
Descartes, René, 35
dice, 5-6, 9-11, 15
dimensions, 33, 40-42
dinosaurs, 42

E
Egypt, ancient, 7, 21
encryption, 13
environmental science, 27
extinct animals, 42

F
factorials, 22
four-in-a-row (game), 21

G
game theory, 26-27
game trees, 22-23, 39
Go (game), 18, 23, 28-29
grids, 20-22, 28-36

H
hangman (game), 37

I
investment banking (career), 25

J
Jenga, 19

L
light, in computer games, 41, 43
lotteries, 12-15

M
magic 15 puzzles, 33

magic squares, 30-31
Minecraft, 40, 42
Monopoly (game), 24-25
Monty Hall problem, 16-17
motion capture, 42-43
multiplication, 9-10, 13, 22, 29
multiverse, 39

P

patterns, 5, 18, 20-21, 25, 29, 30-33, 35-37
percentages, 8, 12-13
Planet Zoo, 40
prisoner's dilemma, 27
probability, 6-9, 13, 16-17, 19, 25-26, 37
pseudo-randomness, 15
psychology, 16

R

radioactive decay, 13, 15
raffles, 7, 12-13, 16
randomness, 7, 13-15
ray tracing, 41
risk management (career), 10
Rome, ancient, 21
Rubik's cubes, 33

S

scores, 5, 10-11, 36-37
Scrabble, 36
security keys, 13
Sevens (game), 11

simulation games, 39
Shannon, Claude Elwood, 23
sharks, 13
Snakes and Ladders, 7
sudoku, 32-33

T

text prediction, 37
three-dimensional (3D) puzzles, 33
tic-tac-toe, 5, 19-22, 28-29
time, in computer games, 40, 42
two-dimensional (2D) computer games, 40

V

video games. *See* computer games

W

World War II, 23

Z

Zelda, 40

Glossary

arithmetic (uh RIHTH muh tihk)—simple math operations of adding, subtracting, multiplying and dividing

billion (BIHL yuhn)—one thousand million (1,000,000,000)

coordinates (koh AWR duh nihts)—pair of numbers, or numbers and letters, that give the "address" of a point on a plan or graph. Three coordinates can specify a location in three-dimensional space.

data (DAY tuh)—raw facts and figures that are processed with math to produce information

encrypting (ehn KRIHPT ing)—converting to a code to keep information secret

factorial (fak TAWR ee uhl)—the result of multiplying together all the numbers beneath a figure, down to 1. For example 4 factorial (4!) is 4 × 3 × 2 × 1.

game theory (gaym THEE uhr ee)—the branch of math that looks at how people make decisions, taking different factors into account

game tree (gaym tree)—a diagram that shows all the possible paths through a series of decisions

hangman—a game that involves guess a word with a specified number of letters, building up the guess one letter at a time. It relies on knowing the likelihood of one letter following another or of letters being grouped together.

interest (IHN tuhr ihst)—money charged on a loan. If someone borrows $100 at 5% interest, they will have to pay back the $100 plus $5 interest.

Jenga—a game that involves removing blocks from a balanced tower without the tower tumbling. Players must figure out how the shapes hold each other up.

motion capture (MOH shuhn KAP chuhr)—technique for making a digital (computerized) record of how an object or person moves as a series of coordinates changing through time

probability (PROB uh BIHL uh tee)—the chance of something happening, expressed as a fraction, decimal fraction, percentage or ratio such as 1 in 4 (= ¼ = 0.25 = 25%)

pseudo-random (SOO doh RAN duhm)—something that looks random but is not mathematically random

psychology (sy KOL uh jee)—science of how people think and behave

radioactive decay (RAY dee oh AK tihv dih KAY)—the change of an atom from one chemical element to another by losing sub-atomic particles or energy

random (RAN duhm)—not following any rules or patterns and so entirely unpredictable

security key (sih KYUR uh tee kee)—series of numbers, or numbers and letters, that are the key to unlocking a digital code and revealing encrypted data

simulation (SIHM yuh LAY shuhn)—a virtual copy of something, such as a scene or process

subconscious (suhb KON shuhs)—mental activity we are not aware of

sudoku (soo DO koo)—puzzle that requires finding missing numbers in a grid of squares to complete a pattern

www.ingramcontent.com/pod-product-compliance
Lightning Source LLC
Chambersburg PA
CBHW061253170426
43191CB00041B/2417